CÁSSIO'S DAY

To my daughter Victoria Maria, who I was expecting at the time the pictures were taken and the text was written. Victoria allowed me to stay healthy and energetic and inspired and encouraged me to climb up and down the hills around Cassiano's village.

First published in Great Britain in 2001 by Frances Lincoln Limited,
4 Torriano Mews, Torriano Avenue, London NW5 2RZ
www.franceslincoln.com

First paperback edition 2003

British Library Cataloguing in Publication Data available on request

ISBN 0-7112-2041-7

Designed by Sophie Pelham

Printed in Singapore

3 5 7 9 8 6 4 2

AUTHOR ACKNOWLEDGMENTS
Special thanks to the following people and institutions for helping to make this book possible:
My husband Richard Davis and Mrs Lilian Davis; Dr Eugênio de Souza Cardoso who dedicated lots
of his time to showing me around, and his mother Dona Estela, who cooked delicious Mineiro food
and looked after me; the Xavante children, Sr Antônio dos Santos, Zilda de Fatima Santos, the sugar mill
of Sr João da Luz, the sugar mill of Sr José Vitor, Fazenda Pomária; Sr Domingos Tótora
of the Oficina de Arte; Danilo, Vanessa, Luís Antônio and Henrique; my friends Nensa, Fafá,
Adriana, and Maria Isabel Barbosa for checking the text; all the people of Maria da Fé
who gave their time and support, and especially the Oliveira family
who made it possible for me to produce this book.

CÁSSIO'S DAY

From Dawn to Dusk in a Brazilian Village

Maria de Fatima Campos

FRANCES LINCOLN

AUTHOR'S NOTE

Probably the first thing that visitors to my country notice is just how mixed Brazilian culture is. It's all the different people who live there – South American Indian, African and European – that help make Brazil such a unique and colourful part of the world.

Cassiano, 'Cássio' to his family and friends, lives in a little village called Maria da Fé in the south-east of Brazil, in the state of Minas Gerais. Most people in the village know each other or are related in some way, and they all live together as one big family.

Maria da Fé is an especially good place to be a child. Cássio and his friends are as free as birds to play outside in the fresh mountain air and waterfalls, and to discover the world around them. When I visited and watched some of the traditional craftsmen at work, I felt a bit like I was stepping back in time. Brazilian life today is mostly very modern and busy, but in Cássio's village people lead much simpler, less hi-tech lives, and I think that makes it extra special.

BRAZIL

Minas Gerais

Cássio is six years old.

He lives with his parents, his older sister Sara and his younger brother Luca. Cássio's mother, Júlia, is an evening-class teacher at the local Adult Education Institute and his father, Heraldo, is a minibus driver. He takes students to the university in Itajubá, the nearby town.

Cássio's grandmother Angelina lives just a few minutes' walk away from Cássio's house. At 6 o'clock, when Cássio is waking up, his grandmother says morning prayers at her *oratório* (shrine). Like many people in Brazil, Cássio and his family are Catholics.

Angelina is holding a rosário (rosary beads) in her hands – each bead represents a single prayer.

2

When everyone is dressed and ready, the family sits down for breakfast. Cássio's father has bought some fresh *pão* (bread) from the bakery near the house. It is still hot from the oven and is delicious with *abóbora* (pumpkin) jam. They also have watermelon, cheese, cake and *pão de queijo* (cheese bread). Cássio drinks orange juice and hot milky coffee.

COFFEE *is grown on plantations all over southern Brazil. There are many different ways to enjoy it – either with milk or cream, or as 'cafezinho', which is very strong, as 'filter' or 'cappucino' coffee, or even as a refreshing cold drink with ice.*

On his way to school, Cássio stops to watch one of the women in the village making *queijo de minas* (cheese of the mines), the traditional cheese of Minas Gerais state.

MINAS GERAIS *means 'General Mines', and takes its name from the mines in the area that used to be worked for gold, silver and precious stones.*

Queijo de minas is very easy to make. Here the cheese is being moulded into shape and squeezed until all the excess liquid is strained away.

Pão de queijo (cheese bread) is a local speciality and is made from strong *queijo de minas* and *polvilho,* a type of flour.

Next Cássio sees some horses making their way from the plantation to the sugar mill. The panniers on their backs are loaded with sugar cane.

SUGAR *(açúcar) production is an important industry in Brazil and Brazilian sugar is sold all over the world. Sr José makes his açúcar in the old-fashioned way, using traditional machinery and methods.*

The sugar cane arrives at the mill and Sr José breaks it all up to extract the cane juice inside. He pours the juice into a big copper pan so that it can be heated up.

As the juice gets hotter it changes colour from light green to gold and becomes a thick treacle called molasses. Sr José pours the treacle into a trough and beats it with a wooden spoon until it cools down.

At this local mill they specialise in *doce-de-leite* (milk sweets). Milk is boiled with the sugar for a long time and then poured into wooden moulds like these to cool.

Cássio's class begins each day with a few minutes of prayer time.
The class is silent so that everyone can say their prayers to themselves
in their own way.

It's very hot so lessons are outside this morning. The children are learning about the Brazilian Indians, and what life was like for them before the Portuguese came to Brazil and made it their home too.

Cássio's mother has made him some chocolate biscuits as a treat and he shares them with his friends at *recreio* (play time). The snack will keep them going until *almoço* (lunch), usually beans, rice, vegetables and meat.

Cássio doesn't stay inside for long, though. He wants as much time as possible to play football with his friends.

Later on, the class visits a local craft workshop. The artists here make bowls using a special mixture of cardboard and banana tree fibre.

The last lesson of the day is held in the school's *horta* (vegetable garden). Any vegetables that are ready are taken to the school kitchen so they can be cooked for lunch tomorrow.

Cássio and his friend Luís Antônio often push each other home from school in Cássio's *carrinho* (barrow).

They stop off at Sr Élcio's sweet shop and buy some of their favourites, *doce-de-leite* (milk sweets).

When they get back home, Cássio joins his brother, sister and friends playing on the broken tree in the garden.

Cássio and his cousin Henrique soon get tired of the tree, so they go for a ride instead. First they have to cross over the *mata-burro* (cattle-grid), which stops cattle from leaving the farm and eating the flowers and vegetables in the garden.

When everyone gets too hot, they play in the little waterfall to cool
down. Sometimes, during the school holidays, Cássio and his family
go to the seaside. Cássio loves paddling in the waves and making
sand castles.

Before going in, Cássio talks to his friend Sr Antônio, who is making *balaios* (baskets). These balaios will be used as panniers for the horses to carry sugar cane or bananas down from the mountain.

BALAIOS *Basket-making is a traditional Indian craft. Indian people use palm leaf, straw or bamboo to make balaios in different shapes and sizes, and they carry all sorts of things in them, even their children.*

On this *galinheiro* (chicken shed), the farmer has filled some balaios with dry grass so that the chickens can lay their eggs in them. These chickens are called *caipira* (free-range) because they don't have cages and are free to run around.

Cássio's mother has been to the market to buy food for dinner.
While she prepares the meal, Cássio goes upstairs to have a shower
and a rest.

Today is Cássio's father's birthday and the whole family has come to help celebrate. Cássio's mother has cooked beans, rice, salad and beef and Uncle Paulo has brought *guaraná* for everyone to drink. Cássio's mother always cooks extra food in case someone arrives unexpectedly. In Brazil you don't need to ask beforehand – you can just call in.

GUARANÁ is a very popular drink, and tastes best when ice cold. It is made from the seed of the guaranazeiro tree which grows only in the Amazon rain forest.

After dinner, Cássio's great-grandmother tells him the story of the patron saint of Brazil – *Nossa Senhora da Aparecida* – while his parents watch a soap opera on television.

NOSSA SENHORA DA APARECIDA *is difficult to translate but means something like 'Our Lady who Appeared' - because her statue once 'appeared' in the nets of three Brazilian fishermen. The fishermen were amazed when they found her and believed that a miracle had taken place: they caught more fish that day than ever before!*

Even though it is bedtime, Cássio is still full of energy.

He sits up in bed and plays with his wooden truck until his mother comes to kiss him goodnight and turn off the light.

Dorme com Deus, Cássio. (Sleep with God, Cássio).

MORE ABOUT BRAZIL

BRAZIL, THE PAST

Before people knew exactly what the world looked like, explorers used to go on voyages of discovery to conquer foreign lands. That's how Brazil came to be discovered in 1500 AD (about five hundred years ago), by an explorer from Portugal called Pedro Álvares Cabral. Brazil was part of the Portuguese empire for the next three hundred years – and today's Brazilians are reminded of their history nearly all the time because the Brazilian national language is Portuguese.

When the first Portuguese settlers arrived in Brazil, they quickly discovered that it was a good place to grow sugar cane. But it wasn't until news spread that gold had been found in the mines in south-east Brazil that people realised just how much their new country had to offer them.

Apart from gold and silver, another important discovery was the rubber tree in the Amazon rain forest – (imagine a world without tyres or rubber bands!). These days, though, Brazil is probably most famous for its coffee. Coffee is grown in the south, where the climate, rich soil and clean air provide the perfect conditions.

BRAZIL, THE LAND

Brazil is the fifth largest country in the world. It's so vast, it has four different time zones – which means that when it's 9 o'clock in Cássio's village, it's only 7 o'clock in Manaus, the capital of Amazonas state. Most of the country is in a part of the world known as the 'Tropics' so it's hot all year round. It still rains, though, especially in the Amazon 'rain' forest area in the north. People who live near the Amazon river have to build their houses on stilts because it rains so much between January and June that the land is completely flooded.

RELIGION IN BRAZIL

Many people in Brazil are Roman Catholic, like Cássio and his family. The African religions 'Candomblé' and 'Umbanda' are also popular. Every New Year's Eve there's an Umbanda festival for the goddess of the sea, Iemanjá, and people celebrate at the coast and near rivers all over the country.

PEOPLE IN BRAZIL

Modern Brazilians are a mix of three different peoples: European, because of the Portuguese and other Europeans who settled in the country; African, because of the African slaves that the Europeans brought into Brazil to work on their sugar cane plantations; and South American Indian, the people who were living in Brazil before anyone in Europe even knew that Brazil existed. It's all these influences that make Brazil such an interesting and lively place to be. The Brazilian sunshine also helps to make people relaxed and friendly. Brazilians love to be by the sea, to listen to music and to dance, especially the samba that is danced at Carnival time, and capoeira, a kind of combat-dance which the African slaves used to perform. The Brazilian national dish, feijoada (a bubbling stew of pork and black beans), also dates back to slave times. The slaves used to make it from the bits of pig that the slave owners didn't want to eat – like the feet, ears, nose and tail!

LANGUAGE IN BRAZIL

Most people in Brazil speak Portuguese, but the Brazilian Indian tribes also have their own languages. So far experts have counted over a hundred different varieties and there are lots of others they're still finding out about.

Brazil is the only Portuguese-speaking country in the continent of South America – everyone else speaks Spanish. With all their Spanish-speaking neighbours, it's not surprising that most Brazilians can understand a few Spanish words, although they might not be able to spell them. Some people speak 'Portunhol', a type of slang which combines Portuguese (**Portu**guês) and Spanish (Espa**nhol**). The Brazilian government would like more children to learn Spanish formally in school so that it will be easier for Brazil to do business with other countries in South America in the future.

The way a Brazilian person speaks also depends on what part of Brazil they come from. It's a very big country, with lots of regional accents. This means that someone from Cássio's village in the south-east of Brazil would pronounce words quite differently from, say, someone from Salvador, a big city on the northeast coast.

SOME BRAZILIAN WORDS AND PHRASES

oi (oy) – hello

tchau (chow) – goodbye

está bom! (es-*sta* bom) – OK!

Como vai você? (kom-o vie vos-*say*) – How are you?

Qual é o seu nome? (qual *eh* o sell *nom*-ee) – What is your name?

THE PORTUGUESE WORDS IN THE BOOK

abóbora – pumpkin

açúcar – sugar, made from sugar cane which
   is grown all over Brazil

almoço – lunch

balaio – basket

café – coffee

caipira – free-range

Candomblé – a popular African religion

capoeira – a kind of combat-dance

carrinho – toy car

doce-de-leite – milk sweets

Dorme com Deus – 'Sleep with God', a popular
   Brazilian way of saying 'sleep well'

feijoada – Brazil's national dish

galinheiro – chicken shed

guaraná – a soft drink made from guaraná seed

horta – vegetable garden

Iemanjá – the goddess of the sea in African religion

Manaus – the capital of Amazonas state in
   northern Brazil

mata-burro – cattle-grid

Minas Gerais – a state in south-east Brazil

Nossa Senhora da Aparecida – the patron
   saint of Brazil

oratório – a shrine, or a special place for praying

pão – bread

pão de queijo – cheese bread, a speciality food
   of Minas Gerais

Pedro Álvares Cabral – the Portuguese explorer
   who discovered Brazil in 1500 AD

polvilho – a type of flour used to make *pão de queijo*
   (cheese bread), made from the manioc plant

Portunhol – slang which combines **Portu**guês
   (Portuguese) and *Espa***nhol** (Spanish)

queijo de minas – 'cheese of the mines',
   a traditional white cheese

recreio – play time

rosário – a string of rosary beads, often used
   by Catholic people when they are praying

samba – the traditional dance of Brazilian Carnival

Umbanda – an African religion similar to Candomblé

INDEX

African religion 25

African slaves 25

basket-making 18, 19

bedtime 23

breakfast 3

Catholic religion 2, 22, 25

cheese 3, 4–5

chickens 19

coffee 3, 24

craft workshop 12

dance 25

dinner 21

football 11

history 9, 24–25

horses 6

markets 20

meals 3, 10, 13, 20, 21, 25

mines 4, 24

patron saint of Brazil 22

Portuguese people 9, 24, 25

language 24, 26, 27

praying 2, 8

rubber 24

school 8–13, 26

South American Indian people 9, 18, 25

language 26

Spanish language 26

sugar cane 6–7, 24

sweet shop 14

vegetable garden 13

weather 24–25